MILLIONAIRE MINDSET

WHY YOU

SHOULD HAVE IT

ESTHER R. ENGLER

I. Introduction

- What is a millionaire mindset?
- Why is it important to cultivate a millionaire mindset?
- How can a millionaire mindset help you achieve financial success?

II. Understanding Wealth and Success

- Defining wealth and success
- The role of mindset in achieving wealth and success
- Common myths and misconceptions about wealth and success

III. Developing a Millionaire Mindset

- Core principles of a millionaire mindset
- Steps to develop a millionaire mindset
- Overcoming limiting beliefs and negative self-talk

IV. Habits of Successful Millionaires

- Key habits that successful millionaires practice
- Strategies to develop these habits
- The importance of consistency and discipline

V. Building a Strong Financial Foundation

- Creating a budget and sticking to it
- The importance of saving and investing
- Strategies for debt management

VI. Overcoming Challenges and Adversity

- The role of resilience in achieving success
- Strategies for overcoming setbacks and challenges
- Turning failures into opportunities for growth

VII. Giving Back and Making a Positive Impact

- The importance of giving back to others
- Strategies for making a positive impact on the world
- How generosity and kindness can benefit you and others

Conclusion

- Final thoughts on cultivating a millionaire mindset

CHAPTER 1

Introduction

The millionaire mindset is a way of thinking and approaching life that is focused on achieving financial success and creating wealth. It is not just about having a lot of money, but also about developing the mindset and habits that are necessary to build wealth over time.

While many people may believe that wealth and success are simply a matter of luck or inherited privilege, the truth is that anyone can cultivate a millionaire mindset and work towards achieving financial freedom. By adopting the right mindset and habits, you can develop the skills and attitudes that will enable you to create the life and financial stability that you desire.

In this book, we will explore what a millionaire mindset is, why it's important, and how you can develop it. We will also examine the habits and strategies that successful millionaires use to build and maintain their wealth. By the end of this book, you will have a better understanding of what it takes to develop a millionaire mindset and achieve financial success in your own life.

What is a millionaire mindset?

A millionaire mindset is a way of thinking and approaching life that is focused on achieving financial success and creating wealth. It involves adopting a set of attitudes, beliefs, and habits that are conducive to building and maintaining wealth over time.

A person with a millionaire mindset understands the importance of hard work, discipline, and perseverance in achieving financial goals. They are not afraid to take risks, but also understand the importance of managing those risks wisely. They have a strong sense of self-belief and are able to overcome setbacks and challenges along the way.

A key aspect of the millionaire mindset is a focus on growth and learning. Those with this mindset understand that there is always room for improvement and are constantly seeking new knowledge and skills that can help them achieve their financial goals.

In essence, a millionaire mindset is a way of thinking and living that is focused on creating financial freedom and stability. It is not just about having a lot of money, but also about developing the skills, attitudes, and habits that are necessary to build wealth over time.

Why is it important to cultivate a millionaire mindset?

Cultivating a millionaire mindset is important because it can help you achieve financial success and create the life that you desire. Here are a few reasons why:

1. Provides a positive outlook: A millionaire mindset helps you to focus on positive outcomes and possibilities. When you adopt a positive outlook, you are better able to overcome setbacks and challenges along the way.
2. Encourages smart decision making: A millionaire mindset helps you to make smarter decisions when it comes to managing your finances. This means that you are better able to avoid financial pitfalls and make wise investments that will help you build and maintain wealth over time.
3. Increases motivation and discipline: Developing a millionaire mindset requires motivation and discipline. By cultivating these qualities, you are better able to stay focused on your financial goals and maintain the habits that will help you achieve them.
4. Builds confidence and self-belief: A millionaire mindset is built on a strong sense of self-belief and confidence. When you believe in yourself and your ability to achieve financial success, you are more likely to take risks and pursue opportunities that can help you build wealth.

In summary, cultivating a millionaire mindset can help you achieve financial success, make smarter decisions, increase motivation and discipline, and build confidence and self-belief. These qualities can benefit you not just financially, but in all areas of your life.

How can a millionaire mindset help you achieve financial success?

A millionaire mindset can help you achieve financial success in several ways:

1. Goal Setting: A millionaire mindset helps you to set specific financial goals and create a plan to achieve them. By setting achievable and measurable goals, you can stay motivated and on track towards achieving financial success.
2. Financial Discipline: A millionaire mindset encourages financial discipline and prudent money management. You learn to live below your means, save and invest wisely, and avoid debt and unnecessary expenses. This helps you to build wealth over time and achieve financial security.
3. Risk-Taking: A millionaire mindset encourages calculated risk-taking. You learn to identify and evaluate risks and opportunities, and take strategic steps to achieve your goals. By taking risks, you can potentially increase your income and wealth over time.
4. Learning and Growth: A millionaire mindset emphasizes continuous learning and growth. You learn about financial management, investment strategies, and business skills, among others. This helps you to make informed decisions and identify new opportunities for financial success.
5. Persistence: A millionaire mindset encourages persistence and resilience. You learn to stay committed to your goals despite setbacks, failures, and challenges. This helps you to overcome obstacles and achieve financial success in the long run.

In summary, a millionaire mindset helps you to set goals, manage your finances wisely, take calculated risks, learn and grow, and persist in pursuing your goals. These qualities are essential for achieving financial success and building long-term wealth.

CHAPTER 2

Understanding Wealth and Success

To develop a millionaire mindset, it's important to have a clear understanding of wealth and success. Here are some key concepts to consider:

1. Wealth is more than money: While money is certainly an important aspect of wealth, true wealth includes other factors as well, such as good health, strong relationships, and a sense of purpose and fulfillment. Having a well-rounded definition of wealth can help you to create a life that is truly rich and fulfilling.
2. Success is subjective: Success means different things to different people. For some, it may mean financial prosperity, while for others it may mean achieving a specific goal or living a life of purpose and meaning. Understanding what success means to you personally can help you to focus on the areas of your life that are most important to you.
3. Mindset matters: Your mindset plays a crucial role in your ability to achieve wealth and success. A positive, growth-oriented mindset can help you to overcome challenges, stay motivated, and achieve your goals, while a negative or fixed mindset can hold you back.
4. Success requires hard work: While luck and opportunity can certainly play a role in achieving success, hard work and

perseverance are essential. Developing a strong work ethic and a willingness to put in the effort required to achieve your goals is key to achieving success in any area of life.

5. Success is not a solo endeavor: Building wealth and achieving success requires support from others, whether it's through networking, mentorship, or collaboration. Building strong relationships and a supportive network can help you to achieve your goals more effectively.

In summary, understanding wealth and success involves recognizing that wealth is more than just money, success is subjective, mindset matters, hard work is required, and support from others is essential. By adopting these perspectives and focusing on your own goals and values, you can develop a millionaire mindset that will help you achieve financial success and create a fulfilling life.

Defining wealth and success

Defining wealth and success is a subjective and personal matter, as they mean different things to different people. However, here are some common definitions and perspectives to consider:

Wealth:

- Wealth refers to having an abundance of resources, including money, property, assets, and investments.
- It can also refer to having good health, fulfilling relationships, a sense of purpose and meaning, and overall happiness and well-being.

- For some people, wealth means having the freedom to do what they want, when they want, without financial constraints.

Success:

- Success refers to achieving a goal or desired outcome, whether it's in a personal or professional context.
- Success can be measured by different metrics, including financial prosperity, career advancement, personal development, and positive impact on others.
- Success is also subjective, as what constitutes success for one person may not be the same for another.

Overall, both wealth and success are multi-dimensional concepts that involve more than just financial prosperity or achieving a specific goal. Developing a millionaire mindset requires a broader understanding of these concepts and the ability to set meaningful and achievable goals that align with your values and priorities.

The role of mindset in achieving wealth and success

The role of mindset in achieving wealth and success is crucial. A millionaire mindset is characterized by a set of attitudes, beliefs, and habits that enable individuals to achieve their financial and personal goals. Here are some key ways in which mindset can impact wealth and success:

1. Mindset shapes behavior: Our thoughts and beliefs shape our actions and behaviors. A positive, growth-oriented mindset can help individuals to take risks, pursue opportunities, and persist in the face of challenges. Conversely, a negative or fixed mindset can lead to self-doubt, fear, and inaction.

2. Mindset influences decision-making: Our mindset can also influence the way we make decisions. A millionaire mindset encourages individuals to make informed, strategic decisions based on their values and goals, while being open to new opportunities and perspectives. A negative or scarcity mindset, on the other hand, can lead to reactive or impulsive decision-making.

3. Mindset affects resilience: Wealth and success require resilience and the ability to bounce back from setbacks and failures. A millionaire mindset encourages individuals to view failure as a learning opportunity, and to stay persistent in pursuing their goals despite obstacles. A negative mindset, however, can lead to feelings of defeat and discourage individuals from trying again.

4. Mindset shapes beliefs about wealth and success: Our beliefs about wealth and success can impact our ability to achieve them. A millionaire mindset encourages individuals to view wealth and success as achievable and attainable, while a negative mindset may lead to beliefs that wealth and success are impossible or unattainable.

In summary, mindset plays a critical role in achieving wealth and success. A millionaire mindset can enable individuals to take action, make strategic decisions, build resilience, and cultivate beliefs that support their goals. By adopting a growth-oriented mindset and focusing on their values and priorities, individuals can develop the attitudes and habits that are necessary for achieving their financial and personal goals.

Common myths and misconceptions about wealth and success

There are many myths and misconceptions about wealth and success that can hold people back from achieving their goals. Here are some of the most common ones:

1. Wealth and success are reserved for a select few: This is a common myth that suggests that only a small group of people have the talent, intelligence, or luck required to achieve wealth and success. In reality, anyone can achieve wealth and success with the right mindset, habits, and strategies.
2. Wealth and success come from luck or inheritance: While luck and inheritance can certainly play a role in achieving wealth and success, they are not the only factors. Most successful people work hard, make strategic decisions, and persist through challenges to achieve their goals.
3. Wealth and success bring happiness: While financial prosperity and achievement can certainly contribute to happiness, they are not the sole sources of fulfillment. Many successful people struggle with mental health issues, relationship challenges, and other personal struggles. Happiness comes from a variety of sources, including relationships, purpose, and personal growth.
4. Wealth and success are purely individual achievements: While individual effort and talent are certainly important,

most successful people rely on the support of others, such as mentors, peers, and collaborators, to achieve their goals. Building strong relationships and networks is essential to achieving long-term success.

5. Wealth and success require sacrificing personal values: This myth suggests that achieving wealth and success requires compromising personal values, such as integrity or authenticity. However, true success and wealth come from aligning personal values with professional goals and pursuing opportunities that are in line with those values.

By recognizing these myths and misconceptions, individuals can adopt a more realistic and effective approach to achieving wealth and success. Developing a millionaire mindset requires acknowledging that wealth and success are attainable for anyone, that hard work and strategic decision-making are essential, and that building strong relationships and staying true to personal values is critical.

CHAPTER 3

Developing a Millionaire Mindset

Developing a millionaire mindset requires cultivating a set of attitudes, beliefs, and habits that support achieving financial and personal goals. Here are some key strategies for developing a millionaire mindset:

1. Set clear goals: Define your financial and personal goals and break them down into specific, achievable steps. This will help you stay focused and motivated, and make progress toward your goals.
2. Adopt a growth mindset: A growth mindset emphasizes the power of effort and learning, rather than innate talent or abilities. This mindset encourages individuals to embrace challenges, view failure as a learning opportunity, and persist in the face of obstacles.
3. Focus on abundance: A millionaire mindset focuses on abundance rather than scarcity. This means viewing the world as full of opportunities and resources, rather than limited or constrained. Adopting an abundance mindset can help individuals identify opportunities and take action toward their goals.
4. Build strong relationships: Building strong relationships with mentors, peers, and collaborators can provide support, feedback, and valuable insights into achieving financial and personal goals. Networking and collaboration are key to long-term success.

5. Take calculated risks: Wealth and success often require taking calculated risks, such as starting a new business, investing in assets, or pursuing a new opportunity. A millionaire mindset encourages individuals to weigh the potential benefits and risks of a decision, and make informed, strategic choices.
6. Prioritize self-care: Developing a millionaire mindset requires taking care of yourself physically, mentally, and emotionally. Prioritize self-care activities such as exercise, meditation, and hobbies that help you recharge and stay focused on your goals.
7. Continuously learn and improve: Finally, a millionaire mindset emphasizes the importance of continuous learning and improvement. Seek out new knowledge and skills, invest in personal and professional development, and stay open to new perspectives and opportunities.

By adopting these strategies, individuals can develop the attitudes and habits that support achieving financial and personal goals, and cultivate a millionaire mindset that can lead to long-term success.

Core principles of a millionaire mindset

Here are some core principles of a millionaire mindset:

1. Goal orientation: Millionaires tend to be highly focused on setting and achieving goals. They know what they want and they work hard to make it happen.

2. Positive attitude: A positive attitude is a key component of a millionaire mindset. Millionaires tend to have a can-do attitude and believe that they can achieve anything they set their minds to.
3. Persistence: Millionaires are persistent in pursuing their goals, even in the face of setbacks and obstacles. They have a strong sense of determination and are willing to put in the effort required to succeed.
4. Self-discipline: Self-discipline is essential for developing a millionaire mindset. Millionaires tend to have strong willpower and the ability to delay gratification in order to achieve their long-term goals.
5. Continuous learning: Millionaires are often lifelong learners. They are always seeking to expand their knowledge and skills, and they are open to new ideas and perspectives.
6. Risk-taking: Successful millionaires often take calculated risks in pursuit of their goals. They are not afraid to step outside of their comfort zones and try new things, even if it involves some degree of risk.
7. Focus on value creation: Millionaires tend to be focused on creating value for others. They look for ways to solve problems, meet needs, and improve people's lives, rather than simply pursuing their own financial gain.

By embracing these principles, individuals can develop a millionaire mindset that supports their financial and personal goals, and increases their chances of achieving long-term success.

Steps to develop a millionaire mindset

Here are some practical steps you can take to develop a millionaire mindset:

1. Identify limiting beliefs: The first step in developing a millionaire mindset is to identify any limiting beliefs that may be holding you back. These could be beliefs about money, success, or your own abilities.
2. Reframe negative thoughts: Once you've identified your limiting beliefs, work on reframing them into more positive, empowering thoughts. For example, instead of thinking "I can't afford that," try thinking "How can I afford that?"
3. Set clear goals: Set specific, measurable goals for your financial and personal life. Break them down into smaller steps and create a plan to achieve them.
4. Adopt a growth mindset: Embrace a growth mindset by focusing on learning and development. View challenges as opportunities for growth and see failure as a chance to learn and improve.
5. Learn from successful people: Read books and articles by successful entrepreneurs and business leaders, attend seminars and conferences, and seek out mentors who can provide guidance and support.
6. Take calculated risks: Identify opportunities that align with your goals and take calculated risks to pursue them. Don't be afraid of failure, but make informed decisions and be prepared to learn from your mistakes.
7. Practice gratitude: Cultivate a sense of gratitude for what you have and the opportunities available to you. This can help you maintain a positive attitude and stay motivated during challenging times.

8. Focus on value creation: Rather than just focusing on making money, look for ways to create value for others. By solving problems, meeting needs, and improving people's lives, you can build a successful business or career while also making a positive impact on the world.

By taking these steps, you can start to develop the attitudes, beliefs, and habits of a millionaire mindset and set yourself up for long-term success.

Steps to develop a millionaire mindset

Here are some practical steps you can take to develop a millionaire mindset:

1. Identify limiting beliefs: The first step in developing a millionaire mindset is to identify any limiting beliefs that may be holding you back. These could be beliefs about money, success, or your own abilities.
2. Reframe negative thoughts: Once you've identified your limiting beliefs, work on reframing them into more positive, empowering thoughts. For example, instead of thinking "I can't afford that," try thinking "How can I afford that?"
3. Set clear goals: Set specific, measurable goals for your financial and personal life. Break them down into smaller steps and create a plan to achieve them.
4. Adopt a growth mindset: Embrace a growth mindset by focusing on learning and development. View challenges as opportunities for growth and see failure as a chance to learn and improve.
5. Learn from successful people: Read books and articles by successful entrepreneurs and business leaders, attend

seminars and conferences, and seek out mentors who can provide guidance and support.

6. Take calculated risks: Identify opportunities that align with your goals and take calculated risks to pursue them. Don't be afraid of failure, but make informed decisions and be prepared to learn from your mistakes.

7. Practice gratitude: Cultivate a sense of gratitude for what you have and the opportunities available to you. This can help you maintain a positive attitude and stay motivated during challenging times.

8. Focus on value creation: Rather than just focusing on making money, look for ways to create value for others. By solving problems, meeting needs, and improving people's lives, you can build a successful business or career while also making a positive impact on the world.

By taking these steps, you can start to develop the attitudes, beliefs, and habits of a millionaire mindset and set yourself up for long-term success.

Overcoming limiting beliefs and negative self-talk

Limiting beliefs and negative self-talk can be significant barriers to developing a millionaire mindset. Here are some strategies to overcome them:

1. Identify and challenge negative thoughts: Become aware of the negative thoughts and beliefs that hold you back, and challenge them with evidence that contradicts them. For example, if you believe that you are not good enough to

succeed, remind yourself of your past successes and accomplishments.

2. Surround yourself with positive influences: Surround yourself with people who uplift and inspire you, read books and articles that motivate you, and listen to podcasts and videos that help you develop a positive mindset.

3. Reframe negative self-talk: Instead of talking negatively to yourself, reframe your self-talk into positive, empowering messages. For example, if you catch yourself thinking "I'm never going to be successful," replace it with "I am capable of achieving success, and I am taking steps to make it happen."

4. Practice self-compassion: Treat yourself with kindness and compassion, just as you would a good friend. Be patient and forgiving with yourself when you make mistakes, and focus on learning and growth instead of dwelling on failure.

5. Visualize success: Use visualization techniques to imagine yourself achieving your goals and living the life you desire. This can help you overcome negative self-talk and cultivate a positive, success-oriented mindset.

By practicing these strategies consistently, you can begin to shift your mindset and overcome limiting beliefs and negative self-talk, paving the way for a millionaire mindset and long-term financial success.

CHAPTER 4

Habits of Successful Millionaires

Here are some common habits of successful millionaires:

1. Goal setting: Successful millionaires set clear, specific goals for their financial and personal lives. They break these goals down into smaller, achievable steps and create a plan to accomplish them.
2. Continuous learning: Successful millionaires are constantly learning and seeking new knowledge and skills. They read books, attend seminars, and seek out mentors who can provide guidance and support.
3. Time management: Successful millionaires are excellent at managing their time and prioritizing their tasks. They know how to delegate, focus on what is most important, and eliminate distractions.
4. Taking calculated risks: Successful millionaires are not afraid to take calculated risks to pursue opportunities. They assess the risks and potential rewards before making a decision, and they are not afraid to learn from their mistakes.
5. Persistence: Successful millionaires are persistent and resilient. They do not give up in the face of challenges or setbacks, but instead, they use these experiences as opportunities to learn and grow.
6. Healthy habits: Successful millionaires prioritize their health and well-being. They exercise regularly, eat a healthy diet,

and get enough sleep. They also prioritize their mental health and practice self-care.
7. Giving back: Successful millionaires understand the importance of giving back to their communities and making a positive impact on the world. They donate to charity, volunteer their time and resources, and use their success to help others.

By adopting these habits and incorporating them into your daily routine, you can begin to develop the attitudes and behaviors of successful millionaires and set yourself up for long-term financial success.

Key habits that successful millionaires practice

Sure, here are some key habits that successful millionaires practice:

1. Focus on results: Successful millionaires focus on achieving results rather than simply going through the motions. They set clear goals and take action to achieve them, measuring their progress along the way.
2. Embrace failure: Successful millionaires understand that failure is a natural part of the process and use it as a learning opportunity. They embrace failure as a chance to grow and improve, rather than letting it hold them back.
3. Take action: Successful millionaires take action and make decisions quickly. They don't let fear or indecision hold them back, but instead, they trust their instincts and take calculated risks.

4. Build relationships: Successful millionaires understand the importance of building strong relationships with others. They invest time and energy in building meaningful connections with mentors, colleagues, and business partners.
5. Continuously learn: Successful millionaires are lifelong learners. They read books, attend seminars, and seek out new knowledge and skills to help them stay ahead of the curve.
6. Work smart: Successful millionaires work smart, not hard. They prioritize their time and energy on high-value tasks and delegate or outsource lower-value tasks to others.
7. Manage finances effectively: Successful millionaires are effective at managing their finances. They budget carefully, invest wisely, and avoid unnecessary debt.

By adopting these key habits, you can develop the mindset and behaviors of successful millionaires and set yourself up for long-term financial success.

Strategies to develop these habits

Here are some strategies you can use to develop the habits of successful millionaires:

1. Start small: Pick one habit to focus on at a time, and start with a small, achievable goal. For example, if you want to prioritize your health, start by committing to 10 minutes of exercise each day.
2. Build a routine: Create a daily routine that incorporates the habits you want to develop. By making these habits a

regular part of your routine, they will become more automatic and easier to maintain over time.

3. Use positive affirmations: Use positive affirmations to help reinforce your commitment to your habits. For example, if you want to focus on taking action, repeat affirmations such as "I am a decisive person who takes action quickly and confidently."

4. Surround yourself with like-minded people: Surround yourself with people who share your goals and values. This can help provide support, encouragement, and accountability as you work to develop new habits.

5. Use visualization: Visualize yourself engaging in the habits you want to develop. This can help reinforce your commitment and motivation to achieving your goals.

6. Set clear goals: Set clear, specific goals for each habit you want to develop. Make sure these goals are realistic, measurable, and achievable, and set a timeline for achieving them.

7. Track your progress: Keep track of your progress towards your goals and habits. Celebrate your successes and use setbacks as opportunities to learn and adjust your approach.

By using these strategies, you can develop the habits of successful millionaires and set yourself up for long-term financial success. Remember, developing new habits takes time and effort, but with persistence and dedication, you can achieve your goals.

The importance of consistency and discipline

Consistency and discipline are essential components of developing a millionaire mindset and achieving long-term financial success. Here are some reasons why:

1. Builds momentum: Consistently practicing good habits and discipline builds momentum towards your goals. It creates a positive cycle of action, progress, and success, which in turn motivates you to continue taking action.
2. Creates a strong foundation: Consistent and disciplined behavior creates a strong foundation for success. By building good habits and practicing discipline, you establish a solid framework for achieving your goals and maintaining your success over the long term.
3. Develops self-control: Consistency and discipline help develop self-control, which is essential for making sound financial decisions. By exercising self-control, you are better able to resist temptations and make rational, well-informed decisions that support your long-term financial goals.
4. Increases resilience: Consistency and discipline also increase resilience. When faced with setbacks or obstacles, you are better equipped to persevere and overcome challenges, knowing that you have the skills and discipline to succeed.
5. Promotes trustworthiness: Consistency and discipline also promote trustworthiness. When you consistently demonstrate good habits and disciplined behavior, others are more likely to trust and rely on you, whether in personal or professional relationships.

In summary, consistency and discipline are critical components of developing a millionaire mindset and achieving long-term financial success. By practicing these behaviors consistently over time, you can build momentum, create a strong foundation for success, develop self-control, increase resilience, and promote trustworthiness.

CHAPTER 5

Building a Strong Financial Foundation

Building a strong financial foundation is essential for achieving long-term financial success. Here are some key steps you can take to build a strong financial foundation:

1. Create a budget: Creating a budget is the first step towards building a strong financial foundation. A budget will help you understand your income, expenses, and financial priorities, allowing you to make informed financial decisions.
2. Build an emergency fund: Building an emergency fund is an essential part of any strong financial foundation. An emergency fund will provide a safety net in case of unexpected expenses or income loss.
3. Pay off high-interest debt: High-interest debt can be a significant barrier to achieving financial success. Paying off high-interest debt as quickly as possible will free up more money for other financial goals and prevent interest charges from accruing.
4. Invest for the future: Investing for the future is a key component of building a strong financial foundation. Investing in stocks, bonds, or other assets can help you grow your wealth over time and achieve your long-term financial goals.
5. Manage risk: Managing risk is essential for protecting your financial future. This can involve purchasing insurance,

diversifying your investments, and being prepared for unexpected events.
6. Educate yourself: Educating yourself about personal finance and investing is essential for building a strong financial foundation. By understanding financial concepts and strategies, you will be better equipped to make informed financial decisions and achieve your goals.

In summary, building a strong financial foundation involves creating a budget, building an emergency fund, paying off high-interest debt, investing for the future, managing risk, and educating yourself about personal finance. By following these steps and making informed financial decisions, you can build a strong foundation for long-term financial success.

Creating a budget and sticking to it

Creating a budget and sticking to it is essential for building a strong financial foundation and achieving long-term financial success. Here are some steps you can take to create a budget and stick to it:

1. Identify your income: Start by identifying all sources of income, including your salary, bonuses, side hustles, and investments.
2. Track your expenses: Next, track your expenses for a month or two to understand where your money is going. This will help you identify areas where you can cut back and make adjustments.

3. Categorize your expenses: Categorize your expenses into fixed (e.g., rent, mortgage, car payment) and variable (e.g., groceries, entertainment) expenses.
4. Set financial goals: Set financial goals, such as paying off debt, building an emergency fund, or saving for a down payment on a home.
5. Allocate your income: Allocate your income to cover your fixed expenses, financial goals, and variable expenses. Be sure to prioritize your financial goals.
6. Track your progress: Track your progress regularly to ensure you are sticking to your budget and making progress towards your financial goals.
7. Adjust as necessary: As your income and expenses change, adjust your budget accordingly to ensure you stay on track.

To stick to your budget, consider these tips:

1. Automate your savings: Set up automatic transfers to savings accounts or retirement accounts to ensure you are saving consistently.
2. Use cash or a debit card: Consider using cash or a debit card instead of a credit card to help you stay within your budget.
3. Limit impulse purchases: Avoid impulse purchases by creating a waiting period before making non-essential purchases.
4. Be accountable: Share your budget and financial goals with a trusted friend or family member who can hold you accountable.
5. Celebrate your successes: Celebrate your successes, such as paying off debt or reaching a savings goal, to stay motivated and committed to your budget.

In summary, creating a budget and sticking to it involves identifying your income, tracking your expenses, categorizing your expenses, setting financial goals, allocating your income, tracking your progress, and adjusting as necessary. By following these steps and sticking to your budget, you can achieve your financial goals and build a strong financial foundation for long-term success.

The importance of saving and investing

Saving and investing are both important for building wealth and achieving financial success. Here are some reasons why:

1. Emergency fund: Saving allows you to build an emergency fund, which is important for unexpected expenses or financial emergencies.
2. Achieving financial goals: Saving helps you achieve your financial goals, such as buying a home, paying for education, or starting a business.
3. Compound interest: Investing allows your money to grow through compound interest. Over time, the interest earned on your investments can grow significantly, helping you achieve long-term financial goals.
4. Diversification: Investing allows you to diversify your portfolio, spreading out your investments across different asset classes and reducing your risk.
5. Retirement savings: Investing is crucial for building retirement savings. By investing in retirement accounts,

such as 401(k)s or IRAs, you can take advantage of tax benefits and grow your savings over time.

To make saving and investing a priority, consider these tips:

1. Set a savings goal: Set a savings goal, such as saving 10% of your income each month, and automate your savings to make it easier.
2. Prioritize debt repayment: Prioritize paying off debt before investing to reduce interest payments and free up cash flow.
3. Start small: Start small and increase your savings and investments over time as your income and financial situation improve.
4. Educate yourself: Educate yourself on different investment options and strategies, such as index funds, mutual funds, or individual stocks, to make informed decisions.
5. Seek professional advice: Consider seeking advice from a financial advisor or planner to help you develop a personalized investment strategy.

In summary, saving and investing are both important for achieving financial success. By setting goals, prioritizing debt repayment, starting small, educating yourself, and seeking professional advice, you can build a strong financial foundation and achieve your long-term financial goals.

Strategies for debt management

Debt can be a major obstacle to achieving financial success and building wealth. Here are some strategies for managing debt:

1. Create a budget: Creating a budget can help you understand your income and expenses and identify areas where you can cut back on spending to free up more money to pay down debt.
2. Prioritize high-interest debt: Prioritize paying off high-interest debt, such as credit card debt, first. This will reduce the amount of interest you're paying and help you become debt-free faster.
3. Consider debt consolidation: If you have multiple debts with high interest rates, consolidating them into a single, lower-interest loan can make it easier to manage your debt and reduce your interest payments.
4. Negotiate with creditors: You may be able to negotiate with your creditors to reduce your interest rates or create a more manageable payment plan.
5. Use windfalls to pay down debt: If you receive a windfall, such as a bonus or tax refund, consider using it to pay down debt rather than spending it on discretionary expenses.
6. Seek professional help: If you're struggling with debt, consider seeking help from a credit counselor or financial advisor. They can help you develop a personalized debt management plan and provide resources and support to help you become debt-free.

By implementing these strategies, you can effectively manage your debt and move closer to achieving financial freedom and success.

CHAPTER 6

Overcoming Challenges and Adversity

Challenges and adversity are inevitable in life, and they can be especially difficult to overcome when it comes to achieving financial success. Here are some strategies for overcoming challenges and adversity:

1. Develop resilience: Resilience is the ability to adapt to and overcome adversity. By developing resilience, you can learn to bounce back from setbacks and maintain a positive outlook even in difficult times.
2. Set realistic goals: Setting realistic goals can help you stay motivated and focused on your financial objectives, even when faced with challenges. Break down your goals into smaller, achievable steps and track your progress along the way.
3. Stay positive: Maintaining a positive mindset can help you overcome challenges and stay motivated. Practice gratitude, focus on your strengths, and surround yourself with positive and supportive people.
4. Seek support: Don't be afraid to ask for help when you need it. Seek support from friends, family, or a professional counselor or advisor to help you overcome challenges and stay on track.
5. Learn from your mistakes: Mistakes and failures are opportunities for growth and learning. Use them as a chance to reflect on what went wrong and what you can do differently in the future.

6. Be flexible: Flexibility and adaptability are important when it comes to overcoming challenges. Be willing to change course or try new strategies when faced with obstacles.

By developing resilience, setting realistic goals, staying positive, seeking support, learning from mistakes, and being flexible, you can overcome challenges and adversity on your path to achieving financial success.

The role of resilience in achieving success

Resilience plays a crucial role in achieving success, especially when it comes to financial success. Here are some ways in which resilience can help you achieve success:

1. Helps you overcome obstacles: Resilience enables you to bounce back from setbacks and overcome obstacles that may stand in your way. This allows you to stay focused on your goals and continue working towards them, even when faced with challenges.
2. Helps you stay motivated: Resilience helps you maintain a positive outlook and stay motivated, even when things get tough. This allows you to persevere through difficult times and keep working towards your goals.
3. Encourages risk-taking: Resilience gives you the confidence to take risks and try new things, even if there's a chance of failure. This can help you discover new opportunities for success and growth.
4. Helps you learn from mistakes: Resilience allows you to learn from your mistakes and failures. Instead of dwelling

on your failures, you can use them as opportunities to learn and grow, which can help you achieve even greater success in the future.

5. Promotes adaptability: Resilience encourages adaptability and flexibility. This allows you to adjust your goals and strategies when faced with changing circumstances, which is essential for achieving success in a rapidly changing world.

In summary, resilience is essential for achieving success, especially when it comes to financial success. By developing resilience, you can overcome obstacles, stay motivated, take risks, learn from mistakes, and adapt to changing circumstances, all of which can help you achieve your goals and become financially successful.

Strategies for overcoming setbacks and challenges

Setbacks and challenges are inevitable on the path to achieving financial success. Here are some strategies for overcoming setbacks and challenges:

1. Identify the problem: The first step in overcoming setbacks and challenges is to identify the problem. This will help you understand what you're up against and develop a plan of action.

2. Stay positive: Maintaining a positive attitude can help you stay motivated and focused, even in the face of setbacks and challenges. Try to see the situation as an opportunity for growth and learning, and focus on finding a solution.

3. Develop a plan: Once you've identified the problem, develop a plan of action. Break the problem down into smaller, manageable steps and focus on taking action to address each one.

4. Seek advice and support: Don't be afraid to seek advice and support from others. Reach out to friends, family, or a professional advisor for guidance and support.

5. Stay motivated: Setbacks and challenges can be demotivating, so it's important to stay motivated. Focus on your goals and the progress you've made so far, and remind yourself why you're working towards financial success.

6. Learn from the experience: Setbacks and challenges can be valuable learning experiences. Take the opportunity to reflect on what went wrong and what you can do differently in the future.

7. Stay flexible: Sometimes, the best way to overcome setbacks and challenges is to be flexible and adapt your approach. Be willing to adjust your goals and strategies as needed, and try new things to see what works.

In summary, to overcome setbacks and challenges, it's important to identify the problem, stay positive, develop a plan, seek advice and support, stay motivated, learn from the experience, and stay flexible. By following these strategies, you can overcome obstacles and continue working towards financial success.

Turning failures into opportunities for growth

Failures can be discouraging, but they can also provide valuable opportunities for growth and learning. Here are some strategies for turning failures into opportunities for growth:

1. Analyze the failure: Take a step back and analyze what went wrong. This can help you identify the areas where you need to improve and develop a plan for addressing them.
2. Learn from the experience: Look for the lessons in the failure. What did you learn? How can you use this experience to improve your future efforts? By taking the time to reflect on the experience, you can turn the failure into a valuable learning opportunity.
3. Stay positive: Don't let the failure get you down. Stay positive and focused on your goals. Remember that failure is a normal part of the learning process and that every successful person has experienced setbacks along the way.
4. Take action: Use what you've learned to develop a new plan of action. Focus on the areas where you need to improve and make changes to your approach. Taking action can help you regain control and momentum after a failure.
5. Seek support: Don't be afraid to seek support from others. Reach out to friends, family, or a mentor for guidance and encouragement. Surrounding yourself with a positive support system can help you stay motivated and focused on your goals.
6. Try again: Finally, don't be afraid to try again. Use the lessons you've learned to improve your approach and try

again. Remember that every failure brings you one step closer to success.

In summary, turning failures into opportunities for growth requires analyzing the failure, learning from the experience, staying positive, taking action, seeking support, and trying again. By following these strategies, you can use failures as a stepping stone to success and achieve your financial goals.

CHAPTER 7

Giving Back and Making a Positive Impact

Achieving financial success is not just about accumulating wealth for oneself, but also about making a positive impact on others and giving back to the community. Here are some strategies for giving back and making a positive impact:

1. Volunteer your time: One way to give back to the community is by volunteering your time. You can find local organizations that align with your interests and values and offer your time and skills to support their cause.
2. Donate money: Another way to make a positive impact is by donating money to organizations that align with your values. Consider setting aside a portion of your income for charitable giving or donating a percentage of your profits if you are a business owner.
3. Mentor others: Share your knowledge and expertise by mentoring others. This can be particularly impactful for young people or those who are starting out in their careers.
4. Support local businesses: By supporting local businesses, you can help create jobs and stimulate economic growth in your community.
5. Reduce your carbon footprint: Taking steps to reduce your carbon footprint can help protect the environment and create a more sustainable future. This can include things like reducing your energy consumption, using public

transportation or biking instead of driving, and reducing your use of single-use plastics.

6. Use your platform for good: If you have a large following on social media or in your community, consider using your platform to raise awareness about important issues and inspire others to take action.

In summary, giving back and making a positive impact involves volunteering your time, donating money, mentoring others, supporting local businesses, reducing your carbon footprint, and using your platform for good. By incorporating these strategies into your life, you can make a meaningful difference in the lives of others and create a better world for all.

The importance of giving back to others

Giving back to others is important for several reasons:

1. It helps create a sense of purpose and fulfillment: When we give back to others, we feel a sense of purpose and fulfillment. We feel like we are making a positive difference in the world and that our actions have meaning and significance.
2. It strengthens our connections with others: Giving back to others can help us build stronger connections with the people and communities around us. By volunteering our time or donating money, we can meet new people and develop relationships based on shared values and interests.
3. It can improve our mental health: Research has shown that giving back to others can improve our mental health by

reducing stress, increasing happiness, and promoting feelings of well-being.

4. It can inspire others to give back: When we give back to others, we can inspire others to do the same. Our actions can create a ripple effect, inspiring others to make a positive difference in the world.

5. It can create positive change in the world: By giving back to others, we can help create positive change in the world. Whether it's supporting a cause we believe in or helping someone in need, our actions can have a real impact on the lives of others.

In summary, giving back to others is important because it can help us find purpose and fulfillment, strengthen our connections with others, improve our mental health, inspire others to give back, and create positive change in the world.

Strategies for making a positive impact on the world

There are several strategies for making a positive impact on the world, including:

1. Volunteer your time: Volunteering your time is a great way to make a positive impact on the world. You can volunteer at a local charity or organization, or you can volunteer your time to support a cause that you're passionate about.

2. Donate to a cause you believe in: If you're not able to volunteer your time, you can still make a positive impact by donating money to a cause you believe in. Whether it's

supporting a local charity or a global organization, your donations can make a difference.

3. Support environmentally-friendly practices: Supporting environmentally-friendly practices is another way to make a positive impact on the world. You can do this by reducing your own carbon footprint, supporting businesses that prioritize sustainability, and advocating for policies that protect the environment.

4. Practice kindness and empathy: Practicing kindness and empathy towards others is a simple yet powerful way to make a positive impact on the world. Whether it's a small act of kindness towards a stranger or showing empathy towards someone who's struggling, your actions can have a ripple effect that spreads positivity and kindness.

5. Educate yourself and others: Educating yourself and others about important issues and causes is another way to make a positive impact on the world. By staying informed and sharing your knowledge with others, you can help raise awareness and inspire action.

In summary, strategies for making a positive impact on the world include volunteering your time, donating to causes you believe in, supporting environmentally-friendly practices, practicing kindness and empathy, and educating yourself and others about important issues and causes.

How generosity and kindness can benefit you and others

Generosity and kindness can benefit both you and others in several ways:

1. Boosts mood and reduces stress: Acts of kindness and generosity can trigger the release of feel-good hormones, such as serotonin and oxytocin, which can help boost your mood and reduce stress levels. When you make others happy, it can also make you feel good about yourself.
2. Enhances relationships: Acts of kindness and generosity can strengthen relationships and build trust. When you show kindness and generosity towards others, it can improve your relationships with them and make them feel more connected to you.
3. Creates a positive ripple effect: Acts of kindness and generosity can have a positive ripple effect. When you show kindness towards someone, it can inspire them to pay it forward and show kindness towards others. This creates a positive chain reaction that can have a widespread impact.
4. Improves overall well-being: Studies have shown that people who regularly engage in acts of kindness and generosity have better overall well-being and are happier than those who don't. When you prioritize kindness and generosity, it can improve your overall quality of life.
5. Helps create a better world: When more people show kindness and generosity towards others, it can help create a better world. Small acts of kindness and generosity can add up to make a big impact, and can help make the world a more compassionate and caring place.

In summary, generosity and kindness can benefit both you and others by boosting your mood, enhancing relationships, creating a positive ripple effect, improving overall well-being, and helping to create a better world.

Conclusion

In conclusion, cultivating a millionaire mindset is not just about achieving financial success, but also about developing a mindset that promotes personal growth, resilience, and kindness towards others. Key principles of a millionaire mindset include a focus on wealth creation, a willingness to take risks, a positive attitude towards setbacks, and a commitment to giving back to others. By practicing habits of successful millionaires, such as discipline, consistency, and a strong work ethic, and building a strong financial foundation through budgeting, saving, and investing, anyone can develop a millionaire mindset and achieve their financial goals. Additionally, by overcoming limiting beliefs and negative self-talk, and developing resilience and strategies for overcoming setbacks, individuals can overcome challenges and adversity on their path to success. Finally, by prioritizing generosity and kindness towards others, individuals can make a positive impact on the world and create a better future for themselves and others.

Final thoughts on cultivating a millionaire mindset

In summary, cultivating a millionaire mindset is not just about achieving financial success, but also about developing a mindset that promotes personal growth, resilience, and kindness towards others. It involves adopting core principles and habits of successful millionaires, building a strong financial foundation, overcoming challenges and setbacks, and giving back to others to make a positive impact on the world.

Developing a millionaire mindset requires discipline, consistency, and a willingness to take risks and learn from failures. It also involves overcoming limiting beliefs and negative self-talk and developing resilience to overcome setbacks and adversity. By adopting these practices and strategies, anyone can develop a millionaire mindset and achieve their financial goals, while also making a positive impact on their own lives and the lives of others.

Remember, cultivating a millionaire mindset is not just about wealth creation, but also about personal growth, resilience, and kindness towards others. It is a journey that requires commitment and dedication, but it is one that can lead to a fulfilling and rewarding life.